"Sally Sweeney takes you by the hand as a teacher would a student to reveal her life stories and pictures. Her presence is felt on every page she writes. With her, the reader meets down-to-earth people she's known."

Reola Robinson, fellow memoirist

"These reminiscences are recipes for the Joy of Living. They are direct, comic, and moving. Give Sweeney's book to anyone who needs a dose of healing laughter. Give this book to anyone who will savor the recreation of American rural life in the 1920s and '30s through the observations of a little girl who tastes pancakes, runs barefoot in the snow, and learns to spell a naughty word. Sally Sweeney, octogenarian artist, is as charming and impish as her childhood self she so vividly evokes."

Lynda Sexson, Author of *Ordinarily Sacred* and other works

HAYSEED

BY

S.T. SWEENEY

HAYSEED

Published by:
Intermedia Publishing Group, Inc.
P.O. Box 2825
Peoria, Arizona 85380
www.intermedia pub.com

ISBN 978-1-935906-24-7

MEMORIES OF GROWING UP IN NEW YORK STATE DURING THE GREAT DEPRESSION.

I don't know when my parents decided to move the family to Lee Center, New York. It was a town about eight miles from the place where we lived in Fish Creek. I was around eight or nine years old. The man who owned the big, old house we were living in, across from Merritt Pratt's, had found a buyer for it. My folks had to scout around for a place big enough for our large family, and find some work that Pa and the older boys could do. The two older girls, Belle and Mickey, were already working away from home. Maggie, the oldest, was married and had a son, Dick.

I remember the first time I saw the "new house." It wasn't as nice as the house we were leaving with the big wrap-around porch and lots of rooms.

The first thing Pa and the boys moved in was the wood burning cook stove. After they got it set up they started a fire in it. The next thing they moved in was the long dining room table with our assortment of chairs. We has some without backs, some three legged, usually held together with baling wire, benches and a rocking chair or two.

Our homes were much different when we were growing up than they are now. We didn't have electricity or running water. The only heat we had in those big, old, drafty houses was the kitchen wood stove. In fact, it was so cold inside the house we had to scrape the frost from the inside of the windows to see outside.

Some of the neighbors had big round pot-bellied stoves in the living room for extra warmth, but we didn't. On very cold days we would crowd around the stove and roast our bellies or back sides, while the other side was chilled to the bone. I liked to sit in front of the stove with my feet propped up on the oven door to get toasty warm; especially after coming in from ice-skating. (I bought the skates from a friend for fifty cents that I had saved from babysitting. They clamped on the shoe bottoms and had a key to tighten them on.)

The rooms were soon filled with a conglomeration of beds and bedding. Some of the beds were iron with white peeling paint. I remember the bed I had to share with my sister, Mary, and she was a holy-terror. It was brass. The head of it had hollow brass tubes that made music when you plunked on them with your fingers. I would get a swat from Mary for "plunking" when I should have been sleeping. She would threaten, "Sarah, if you do that once again I'll smack you"! Of course I had to do it "one more time." I couldn't let her boss me, and then wham! True to her word, I'd get an eye opener across the face. I would scream, "Ma, Mary is hitting me!" Mary would reply, "Make her behave and go to sleep." I don't remember how we ended up, she either gave up on smacking me or I finally tired of my musical plunking. That night anyway.

I don't remember much about moving in, except we kids would run from room to room looking everything over to see if there were any treasures left over from the former tenants.

There was a steep and narrow stairway that led to an attic. When we kids went whooping up there we found boxes of books, old newspapers, and musty discarded clothing to try on. Lots of good stuff! We also found some spider webs, mice and squirrel nests.

On rainy days we would go upstairs, which was one big room, and rummage through the treasures stored up there. Ma and Pa had a big, square, metal trunk with a domed lid and leather straps on it. Inside was their family album. It was made of purple velvet, with a gold colored clasp. The key to it had been missing for years, thanks to so many snoopy kids. The album held tin type pictures and old photos of grandparents, aunts, uncles from both sides of the family, also some of Ma and Pa when they were young. There was a spyglass made of brass that would telescope in and out. We pretended we were pirates aboard a ship and would yell, "Ahoy me Mates." Even Ma's wedding blouse was in there. It was white lace and so small, she must have been a tiny person when she was a bride. We also had an old clock that looked like a Roman building with columns. It was made of black marble and had lions on each end with rings in their mouths, which were the handles. It didn't work anymore, but we would wind it up to hear it "boing." Best of all was a large wicker baby carriage with a hood. It could also be made into a stroller. We would take turns riding in it and pushing each other around like greased lightening. Don't know what ever happened to it.

The house had two bedrooms and a huge living room, which was used as a bedroom for the boys and Uncle Stillman, Ma's brother, who usually lived with us. We called him "The Rattling Cannon Ball." You'll hear more about him later on.

The kitchen and dining room was one big room. The old iron cook stove, tables and chairs filled it up. There was a long, rusty, iron sink in one corner where the dishes and everything were washed, a stool and shelf to hold the water pail and the wash-dish (a basin used for our personal grooming) was beside it. There was a large pantry off the kitchen for the food stuff, dishes, pots and pans. There was also a big cellar under the house. It was so spooky, dark and damp, I seldom went down there.

Outside the back door of the kitchen was the garage attached to the house. Our old flivver of a car, an old STAR car, was kept there along with the firewood and assorted "good" junk.

A little lane behind the garage meandered down and around to the "out-house" or "back house" as we called it. It was a three-holer, about as big as the well house and had a half moon cut in the door for ventilation. We would sit out there and read the Sears and Monkey Ward's catalogues, which were also used for toilet paper. So much for that delicate subject.

There was a cluster of hollyhocks growing around it too. At least you never had to ask where IT was. Just follow the hollyhocks!

We had one coal oil lamp for light, so our bedtime was usually when the sun went down. The kids who had homework for school were allowed to stay up and study by the lamp light.

Also on the property was a big, old barn, some tumble down sheds and chicken houses. We had a great time getting to know this house.

The hand water-pump was in front, across from the kitchen. It had a long handle to pump the water for household use.

Pa rented this house from Charlie Lemon. He and the older boys worked for Charlie on his big farm a couple miles down the road from us. Charlie also raised beans for the canning factory. For a penny a pound, the kids who were big enough got out and picked beans from sun-up to sun-down. I was lucky if I even made a dollar a day. It was hard work bending and picking all day and lugging the gunny sack to the end of the row. My brothers, Buck and Tyke, worked in the canning factory in the summer.

Working in the fields was hard work, but fun. We met neighbors from miles around. Whole families were in the fields. When the mothers and fathers were with the kids, I imagine a lot more beans were picked. The ones who got the most money for the day were called "Bean Hogs." Mary, Jack and I were the "Bean Pickers" in the family

Our nearest neighbors were the Wintertons. They had three boys and three girls, who weren't quite as rowdy as we were. They had a dairy farm across the lot from our place. When Pa and Ma went to town, us kids would climb up on top of the big barn and yell obscenities and make faces at the Winterton kids. We also used to run down the roof of the barn to the eaves, and scare the bejesus out of them, thinking that we would fall. There must have been a special angel looking out for us.

About a mile further up the road lived the Dust family. Bill, his wife, Pearl and their two children, Leta and Billy all knitted their own sweaters, socks, mittens and caps. In fact, I think all of their clothing was homemade. I couldn't get over the sight of men knitting. When they moved away to another town, Bill sold his 105 acre farm to my folks.

That was our first real home.

The first thing my sister Mickey did when we moved into that house was to stick her finger in the light socket to see if the electricity was "on." There was just a naked light bulb hanging in the kitchen and dining room. We had a blast turning the lights on and off 'til Ma got after us. After Mickey got shocked we left it alone.

The MacDonald family lived about a mile further up the road from us. They also had a slew of kids, all around our ages. And the Bill Corr family lived directly cross-lot from our home. They had a big family also. Anyone who only had one or two kids was considered "rich" by the rest of us.

The Main Street in Lee Center was paved, but all the rest were dirt or gravel roads. Our road was dirt and in the spring when the ground thawed, the tire ruts would get so deep and full of clay that the cars could no longer run on them. Then they would make new trails through the pastures. Occasionally, the state would send crews through with blades and scrapers to dig out the ruts and even the roads out for travel.

I liked the roads in the hot summer. They would be as hard and smooth as marble. Big maple and apple trees lined the roads and it was a pleasant walk to school and town.

Wild roses grew in the fields along the roads. Sometimes there would be remnants of an old homestead and our imagination would be sparked as to who they were in that long ago time before we moved there.

Thomas Children and Friends

Lee Center, N.Y. Grade School

Lee Center Town Barn, Grist Mill
Mrs. Robinsons' House on Hill

HALLOWEEN

When I was small Halloween was a spooky, shivery night. Why, I don't know! The only daring thing that I can remember doing was running down the road and back with my bare feet in the snow. The older kids had dared me to do it. They told ghost and goblin stories and usually ended up scaring the day lights out of me.

An Old Polish couple, Mr. and Mrs. Pija (Pronounced Pie), lived down the road from us when we lived in Fish Creek. The bigger neighbor kids, Johnnie Stemkoski, Louis Synic and of course my older brothers, used to push her outhouse over. One Halloween night she got there before the pranksters and moved it back a couple of feet. When the kids sneaked up to give it a push, were they ever surprised! Yuck! What a mess they were standing in! Mrs. "Pie" had tricked them. She had a good laugh.

During another Halloween, the teenage boys in Lee Center, Gratt Lemon, "Jiggs" Andregg, Chet Sycezyk, "Pickles" Maucomber, and of course my brothers, stole Charlie Lemon's wagon. Once they got it they took it up on Main Street, dismantled it, climbed up on the roof of the Protestant church. With ropes and a lot of help hoisted it up piece by piece and reassembled it, astraddle the roof.

Imagine the surprise of the town Elders when they saw the wagon up there the next morning and wondering what bit of ingenuity got it up there. A lot of devilment was done in our little town. The outhouse from behind the school was dragged to and deposited in front of Clyde Felshaw's drug store on Main Street.

Many of the dairy farmers found their milk cans high up in the maple trees. The Halloween pranksters really earned their reputations that night! They also went to the graveyard and prowled around the head stones and making weird sounds at any unwary passers-by. What a delicious, scary feeling we got if we happened to be out on that night.

My mother would pretend that she didn't see us younger kids soaping the windows, but the next day we had a job of washing them with vinegar water and shining them with newspapers. One way to get the windows washed!

HALLOWEEN

MEALTIME AT OUR HOUSE

Seldom, if ever, did we have a meal without the whole family being together. When Ma would yell "It's on the table," we would drop whatever we were doing and go inside, wash up and stand behind our chairs at the table. No one was allowed to sit until Pa sat in his place first.

The food, plates, and meal were next to Pa at the head of the table. He would parcel out the food on each plate and it was handed around the table to each person. The ones who worked got the most.

Sometimes we would get the giggles. Someone would "cut the cheese" or sneak one out... Pa would tell the culprit to go outside and run around the house three times before we could finish our meal. We all had to sit at the table until everyone was finished. Then we would ask if we could be excused. So we did have some manners in spite of such a noisy, rowdy family. There were never any left-overs; I think we ate anything that didn't move.

If anyone missed the call to come to the table, they had to wait until the next meal.

Ma was a good whistler. She would put two fingers in her mouth and let out the shrillest whistle you ever heard. No matter where we were we could hear her. That is how she called us when there was something she really, really wanted us for.

SUMMER SALESMEN

In the spring and fall Rawleigh and Watkins' men would come around in their horses and wagons, with medicine and cures for man and beast. The medicines that I remember most were red liniment to rub on animals' sore legs etc, and a sure-fire cure for arthritis, bursitis, leg cramps and every ache and pain imaginable. It also made a delicious hot drink for stomach aches. You just took one teaspoon of red liniment and mixed it with sugar, milk and hot water. I loved it! I also remember the big tin box of Carbolic salve, which was used for people and animals alike. They also carried spices, vanilla, baking soda and powder and extract to make a kool-aid type of refreshing drink. My mother would often trade a hen or two in exchange for the merchandise she needed.

The ragman would come through the area during spring and fall house cleaning time. Any scrap of rag we could find, we would save for him. There weren't many rags to be found, as we all wore hand-me-downs until they were patched, re-patched and in shreds before the ragman came. He would give us a couple of pennies for our loot and we were really rich for awhile. We carried the pennies around for days counting them over and over until we lost them or Pa would con us out of them so he could buy himself his package of "Little Yara" chewing tobacco, which he was addicted to and his only vice that I knew of.

The Tinker would come just once a year. We could hear him for a mile and a half down the road before he got to our place. It was usually hot and dusty and I can still hear the pots and pans and other paraphernalia clanking together, as his horse and wagon jostled over the rutted, tree lined road. He could sharpen anything that needed it, fix holes in Ma's kettles, wash tubs or frying pans, which the older generation called "spiders." Ma also bartered chickens or eggs in exchange for his wares.

I remember one time when he traded her an aluminum "waterless cooker" for two hens. It was beautiful! It was the first *new* kitchen utensil that I had ever seen. It was so shiny I could see my reflection in it. It was huge; must have held two or three gallons. We used to peel enough potatoes to fill it for a meal for our large family. "Just add a cup of water and simmer on the back of the stove until the food was done. Guaranteed not to burn or scorch!" I do remember eating a lot of scorched oatmeal, beans, potatoes etc. though.

Ma could sure make the most delicious vegetable soup we had ever tasted. Pa called it "Lub-Scouse" which is the Welsh name for it. A big pot of homemade soup and bread, fresh baked from the oven. That was my idea of HEAVEN.

When I was eight or nine years old, I wanted to learn to make bread so bad! It looked like such fun, sifting the flour, watching the yeast rise in the jar of tepid water and sugar. Then getting my hands in all of that gummy dough and kneading and punching it until it was all mixed up and smooth. We had an enormous bread pan, also used as a dishpan, that would take eight big sifters of flour, a handful of salt, some bacon grease, when we had it, and the yeast and enough water (potato water if we had it) to make the dough. Then we'd cover it with damp, clean flour sacks which were also used as dish towels. Finally, we'd put a blanket over it to keep it warm so it would rise over night. In the morning, I would punch it down and let it rise a second time, then make loaves and let them rise in the warming ovens on the wood stove. It took a lot of wood to keep the oven hot enough for baking. The ovens didn't have temperature gadgets on them, so the baking was done by feel. When the bread would get brown on top, we would take it out of the pans and turn it upside down so the bottom could brown too. We would give it a couple of "thumps" to see if it sounded done. It would yield up to eight loaves of brown, crusty bread that would "stick to your ribs," so Pa said. Occasionally, on mornings when the bread wasn't ready to bake, Ma would fry it for us. Mmmmmmmmmm, that was so GOOD! That was probably the forerunner of the "Elephant Ears" we get at fairs nowadays.

Mary, Jack and I took turns making the bread as it had to be made every day. I soon learned to hate my turn, when it wasn't fun anymore. It was work! I was so small that I had to put the bread pan on two chair seats to be able to punch and knead the bread. So much for my cooking talents!

SUMMER SALESMEN

LIZZIE LOWER

I think everyone has a certain character that sticks in their mind from their childhood. Mine was "Lizzie Lower." She and her husband, Harry, moved directly across the road from our house in Henry Suitor's old home, when we lived in Fish Creek. Lizzie was a very small, thin, mousy person. Her hair was straw colored and she parted it in the middle and piled it up in a mammoth bun on the back of her head. She was as nervous as a jay-bird and had a habit of tweaking her lower lip. She had a lot of warts or moles on her pasty, white face. She also had a speech impediment which I found fascinating. Her "R's" came out sounding like "W's" or "U's". She would call Harry, "Hawwy"—I loved it!

"Hawwy" would give me and my brother Eddie,

piggy back rides. He'd gallop through the house with us sitting on his shoulders and hanging onto his several chins, for dear life. He was as rotund and fat as Lizzie was thin and small. Although Lizzie was my idol at that time, she was also the cause of many of my disciplinary problems at home.

We, being her only neighbor for miles; anything that happened at our house was a source of excitement for her. She would often call me over to her house and ask me what was going on at my home. I, being only four years old and having not learned to fib yet, would tell her what ever she wanted to know. Then I couldn't figure out why I got my mouth slapped when I got home and had to stand behind the hot kitchen stove until I was told that I could move.

Lizzie also taught me how to spell; which resulted in another session behind the kitchen stove. CHILD ABUSE!!!! I liked to visit her on rainy days. She usually did her ironing then. She had *real curtains* on the windows. One day, I was over there when she was ironing her living room curtains and trying to hang them up. They must have been wide windows, because I can picture her standing on a ladder and getting one side of the rod into place and every time she would try to get the other side up the whole shebang would fall on the floor. SHIT! She would yell. S-H-I-T shit! Over and over until she got them up.

I remember running home yelling "Ma, I can spell! I can spell!" "Lizzie taught me." So I spelled s-h-i-t, SHIT for Ma. Well! I thought I had been hit by a lightning bolt! I got a good swat right in the mouth with the back of her hand, her left hand, the one with the wide gold wedding band on it. So after that whenever Lizzie had a spelling bee with herself, I never mentioned it to Ma.

There was a creek in the field behind Lizzie's house. I can still see it! There was a path lined with trees going to it. I imagine it was a cow trail. My older brothers and Johnnie and Louie used to go swimming in it. Sometimes Mary and I would tag along. We never could learn to swim. The boys taught us how to swim "Duck style." As soon as our heads would come up for air they would duck us under the water again. Our Guardian Angels must have been watching over us then, Big Time!

One of the boys found a big black water snake, which they killed and put into a hollow piece of bark off of a tree limb. I can remember them calling Lizzie out to see what they had. She came out of her kitchen door, wiping her hands on her apron. They tilted the bark and the snake shot out at Lizzie's feet. Lizzie did a royal jig and tore into the house yelling: "Hawwy, Hawwy!" at the top of her lungs. I chalked one up for the boys; they got the licking that time!

The old house we lived in had long windows from the ceiling almost to the floor. We didn't have a porch but there was a slab of concrete in front of the windows. I remember standing out there and pulling my panties down and looking at my butt's reflection in the windows. I thought it was pretty neat! Of course I'd catch the "old harry" and get swatted when Ma caught me.

LIZZIE LOWER

OUR BARN FIRE

This was when Henry Suitor and his wife and son still lived across the road from us in Fish Creek. Ma had walked the mile or so to the Fish Creek one-room school, with the kids who were practicing for a Christmas play. It was cold and crisp outside, the snow crunched under their feet and a big silver moon was in the sky. Eddie and I had been put to bed upstairs. All I can remember was being awakened by fire engine sirens and a lot of commotion in the yard.

Our barn was on fire!! Pa and a couple of the boys were out in the barn catching the chickens and cooping them up in an old car. I think it had side curtains and I know he had to crank it to get it started.

When the flames spread to the house roof, they got Eddie and me from our room and sent us over to Suitor's place. I remember running back home and going upstairs to get my new shoes out from under the bed. They were the first new shoes I could ever remember having.

The fire engine wasn't putting out much water and I heard one of the boys saying "I can pee a bigger stream than that!" I guess he could have, as the fire engine ran out of water. The firemen took the quilts from our beds and soaked them in what they thought were big milk cans full of water on the back porch, and putting them on the roof, only to blaze and burn like fuel added to the fire. It turned out that the milk cans were full of maple sap which was collected to make maple syrup and candy when there was enough for "sugaring."

Buck ran to the school house and yelled "Ma! Ma! The whole place is on fire!" Ma ran, walked and rolled all the way home. We stayed at the Suitor's house that night. In the morning I had my first taste of pancakes. I'll never forget the heavenly aroma of bacon, pancakes and coffee perking on the stove. I ate pancakes with maple syrup until my belly ached and I had to roll on the floor for relief.

A few days later, when Eddie and I came downstairs on the morning of December 22nd, Ma was still in bed. She called us in and asked if we'd like to have a doll for Christmas. I didn't want a doll, but I sure did want a table, chairs and dishes. Then she lifted the blanket and showed us the "doll" she had for us. A real live one named Esther. She let us both hold her. I was in seventh heaven for a week. Not over the new baby, but because the stork had *actually been in our very own house.* Sophie and Johnnie Stemkoski came to see the baby and Johnnie was so surprised to see that she had her eyes open already and she was only a few days old.

I had a piece to speak at school for Christmas Eve, it was something about a doll or whatever, and Ma let me hold Esther on my lap on the stage while I recited it.

I do remember one poem I had to recite on the stage at school. It was before I started school, so I must have been about four years old.

OUR BARN FIRE

A LITTLE FAIRY DUTCHMAN

A Little Fairy Dutchman
Went to take a bath
He hung his little britches
On a stem along the path.
Some other little fairies
Played a joke on him.
He came along the path and picked the little
stem.
What ever did that little Fairy Dutchman do?
Why, he went right back and swam
'Til other britches grew.

The audience loved it, and even after I was grown, the older folks always called me "Leather Britches" when they would see me. I must have made quite an impression on them.

I was always drawing and coloring pictures with crayons. I must have been pretty good as Ma would save the brown paper the groceries and just about everything from the stores was wrapped in. She would press it smooth with the old sad iron, which had to be heated on the stove; sew it together with yarn to make books for me. She must have noticed the artistic ability I had. I could draw just about anything I put my mind to. I think she was the guiding force behind my getting into the world of art. Thank you, Ma!

BOYD'S HILL

Up the road from Lizzie Lower's was a big hill where the Boyd family lived. There was Roger and Dora, their daughter June was around my older brother's age and she went to the Fish Creek School too. They also had a daughter named Doris. I don't know what her affliction was, but she was unable to go to school or play with anyone. Her mother had to take constant care of her. Their hill seemed like a long walk from our house and that is where the older kids went "sliding down hill." I remember when Tom and the older boys made a toboggan out of some old tin. Mary went with them to try it out. I don't know what happened, all I know is that she didn't stay long. The toboggan tipped over and she got hurt. When she showed Ma where, it was a big hunk torn out of her behind by the ragged edge of the toboggan. I'm sure she carried that scar with her the rest of her life.

Lizzie Lower used to go "sliding down hill" with the kids. She must not have been as old as I thought she was.

One time, when it was very cold out and my hands and feet felt like they were freezing, Jack and I stopped at Boyd's house on our way home from school and asked Dora if we could come in until I got warm. Dora said, no, we didn't have too much farther to walk to our own house and she was sure I wouldn't freeze to death if we just kept on going.

She was a very odd woman; she probably thought we would contaminate Doris.

Stringing Fart Skins

A short ways up the road from the school house lived Mr. Rood. He had a housekeeper who's name was Mary. I liked to visit them occasionally. He sounded kind of grumpy, but he really wasn't. I didn't realize it at the time, but he must have had a stroke or something. He was always sitting in a big chair by the stove. I'd say, "What ya doing Mr. Rood ?" and he would reply, "Stringing fart skins." Mary would soak big beans which must have been dried limas, although I had never seen beans like that before. He would slip the skins off them and string them together with a needle and thread. There were a lot of them hanging from the ceiling. Never could figure that one out.

Across the dirt road from Mr. Rood, lived Mrs. Brown. I don't know if there was a Mr. Brown or not. Probably her brother or older son lived with her. She had the prettiest apple tree in her yard. Eddie and I would climb up the tree and get some apples. We never thought of swiping anything. She would come outside and make us get out of the tree and give her the apples. "Dang

Old Biddie."

Further on up the road past the Roods lived the Nemos. The older boys worked for Mr. Nemo when he did the butchering. They would save the blood from the animals and make blood sausage. Ma said we were never to eat anything made of blood. But I tasted it once and it was good. Mr. Nemo was very strict with his family. They couldn't go visiting or play with anyone. Just to school and back. I think Mrs. Nemo was a lonely person. I would stop in to visit her once in awhile and she seemed glad to have someone to talk to. She would give me a big slab of cake, but it never had sugar in it.

About a mile up the road from Nemo's was where the road came to a "T." I don't know where the right road went, but the left went up to Stemkoski's. They had a beautiful home and farm. I loved to go and visit them. They also had a piano in the parlor they would let me try to play. Sophie could play it really well and Johnnie would sing. They made several tin records together.

Mrs. Stemkoski would grab a chicken, put its head on the ground and hold a broom over its neck with her feet, and pull its head off. I swore I'd never eat chicken after I saw that. But when it was cooking and she dished it up for dinner, it was great! I loved it.

I would visit Sophie and stay the weekend with her. She would swipe her Pa's tobacco and some roll up papers; we would make cigarettes and smoke them when we went upstairs to bed at night. She would open the windows a crack and we would lay on the floor under them so the smoke would go outside. Then we'd rub the ashes into the rug, as Sophie said it would keep the wool rugs from getting moths. Sophie was very short with a crooked spine and a hump on her back. She and all of her family were my lifelong friends. Her folks were my second set of parents.

Further on up the road from the Stemkoski family lived the Synic family. I never did venture that far up the road.

Now that I mentioned "smoking," I remember when we went to the Fish Creek School, most of the kids would get there before Miss Greggains did. The boys would open all the windows and get the pencil shavings out of the sharpener and roll them up in paper and make cigarettes. We would all get a "puff" on them, so we wouldn't tell. We used "penny pencils" made of cedar wood. Wonderful aroma. Don't remember the taste…

THE CRANK UP RECORD PLAYER

The only music we had at our house was an old record player that took big round hard rubber records. We only had one or two of them. Sometimes the Jehovah Witnesses would come by and bring some religious records to play, along with their other pamphlets etc. trying to get Ma and Pa to become one of them. One song that I remember distinctly was "The Razors are Flying Through The Air." That was about the only music we had until Pa got a radio, which was run on batteries and Pa rigged a wind-mill up to the roof of the house to charge the batteries and also provide electricity for a single light bulb we had hanging from the ceiling. We were getting "up in the world those days." Sometimes, when the wind blew really hard, Pa would have to put the brakes on the wind-mill or I'm sure it would have torn the roof off of the house.

THE CLARKS

Down the road from us lived the Clark Family. There was old Mrs. Clark, Andy who was fat (in fact he played Santa Clause at school after our Christmas plays), Frankie, he must have had polio or something when he was little because his back was bent and his legs were twisted. Yet he was tall in spite of his handicaps. He used a cane to walk, and boy could he ever play the accordion! Their sister, Mabel played the old organ they had.

Mrs. Clark used to give Eddie and me sugar cookies for bringing their cows home at milking time. They kept the cows pastured in a meadow way up the road by our place. Those were the best cookies! We hardly ever got any at home. So, when we got hungry for cookies we would go and round up the cows and take them to the Clarks. Sometimes it was in the middle of the afternoon. We soon learned that was a "no no."

Usually on weekends, Pa, Ma and most of us kids would troop down to the Clarks in the evening after the chores were done. It was usually getting dark and the stars were coming out. Frankie would play his accordion and Mabel played the organ and everyone would sing. Those were very good times. My father had a beautiful tenor voice and he loved to sing. After our song fests were over Mrs. Clark gave us cookies and cider, then we would walk back home. Pa would let me ride on his shoulders and Ma would carry Eddie. I don't remember going down so much after Esther was born.

MY SALESMAN DAYS

When I was about seven or eight years old, I would send for Cloverine and Rosebud salve. They smelled heavenly and I think they were used for chapped hands and as a face moisturizer.

I got a prize for selling it if I met their quota. I really don't remember what that was, but it was probably a couple dozen tins of it.

I walked miles to all of the neighbors, and most of them bought from me.

MY SALESMAN DAYS

POLITICIANS

All I can remember about voting time was when whoever was running for office would come around to all of the houses they could find on the back roads etc.; I am sure they never knew that we existed before that. They had Baby Ruth candy bars for the kids and the women and cigars for the men, to get their votes at election time. We kids looked forward to that.

I would always go cross lots to my school teacher, Bessie Greggains' home. They had a big farm and her parents were so nice. I remember they usually had apple pie with a slice of cheddar cheese on it. They would give me a big slice and it was wonderful. I didn't care much for the cheese on it though. Never saw anyone serve it like that before. I don't know if I went there to "really" sell the salve or for the apple pie hand out.

I remember the prize I got for selling the salve. It was a silver ring with a rounded top that opened and there was a little ball of cotton with perfume on it placed in the top. How I loved that ring.

I still had it when I was older, but my brother Buck conned me out of it. He couldn't afford an engagement ring for his girlfriend, Jeannette Austin. I guess it worked for the time being, as they ended up getting married.

Moving on again.

We moved from across from Lizzies' to a big house across the road from the Merritt Pratt place. He was separated from his wife and lived alone with his three children. Sonny, Jane and Olive. We finally had neighbors to play and fight with. This was also the first time I ever saw a *real doll* in person, instead of in a catalogue. Janie and Olive each had a beautiful doll with teeth, flirty eyes, jointed legs and arms, curly hair and they cried "Mama." I was fascinated! They would let me dress and undress them. How I dreamed of having a doll of my very own. I would close my eyes and spin around and around and hope for one. I pretended when I opened my eyes, it would be there. But it never was!

This old house had a second floor where I slept with Belle and Mary. I was scared of the dark and it was too cold to run out to the "back-house" in the night when nature called, so I would open the window and stick my behind out and pee. I didn't think anything about it until spring time came and Ma noticed a brown streak running down the side of the house under the window. When she asked who had been "peeing" out the window, I owned up to it. I don't know if I got a licking or not, but I didn't do it again.

The "Powers that be" in the county decided

there were too many un-licensed dogs in the area which wasn't making any money for the local government, as the owners couldn't afford to buy dog licenses. Mr. Peters, the dog catcher, came to the area miles from Lee Center to check on any un-licensed dogs and give warnings to get them licensed "or else."

Our dog was a small, black and white mongrel named Tippy. The Pratt's dog was named "Beppo." When Mr. Peters came around the second time and the dogs still didn't have a tag, he shot Beppo right in front of us kids. We were frantic for days. One morning, we heard a gun shot before we got up. When we arose and called for Tippy she never came. Pa had taken her out to the woods and shot her so we wouldn't see it. That was our first encounter with politicians and death!

MARY, ME AND OUR EASTER BASKET HATS

Usually on Decoration Day, Mary and I would walk the few miles from Lee Center to Taberg to march in the parade through the town and put flags on the Veteran's graves in the cemetery. What urged us to go was a triple decker ice cream cone from one of the stores in Taberg, which gave one to each kid at the end of the parade. Ma had been in Rome, shopping, a few days before this and brought us home a wonderful surprise... so she thought! What a disappointment when we were presented with our new straw hats. Ugh! They looked like upside down Easter Baskets. Mine was dark blue with a green and purple band. I don't remember what Mary's was like, but then and there we vowed that we WOULD NOT wear them. Ma had other ideas. Either wear them or stay home! It was a hot day, so we wore the hats. Period! For about half an hour, that is. Then we hid them in the bushes along the road and went merrily on our way. After the parade and the ice cream cones, (mine was a maple walnut dip and a strawberry dip) which were eaten slowly, making them last as long as possible, we met a lot of folks from around home at the parade and got a ride home. We were so tired and hot after the long walk and parade, we forgot all about our hats. Imagine our surprise when we got home to find our hats on the kitchen table and a very, very mad mother. I don't remember if we got switched that time or not, but I never forgot those blasted straw hats!

MY FIRST DAY OF SCHOOL

When I was a little over five years old I had my first day of school. I felt so grown up going to school with the bigger kids. They had already taught me to read, write and do arithmetic and the times tables etc. at home. I had visited the school before and knew all the kids who went there.

It was a one-room school with Kindergarten through the eighth grade. The teacher's desk was on a stage in the front of the room in front of the black board. The stage is where we had our Christmas plays. We also used to go up there to do some of our oral lessons. There was even a dunce stool up there where the fool of the day got to sit.

A big, black, pot bellied stove provided the heat in the winter and on cold days. Andy Clark would deliver the wood. I think he had a crush on Miss Greggains too. How we would snicker when he would show up.

I was soon promoted to the second grade. I would get so bored I would do the lessons for all of the grades.

A lot of times Miss Greggains would pick me to clap the blackboard erasers. I'd take them outside and clap them together until the chalk was gone. I really think she conned me into doing it, because no one else wanted the job. She would catch me when I was playing and have me ring the school bell at recess time, meaning that recess was over and it was time to go back to our studies. The older kids would get mad at me when I got to ring the bell.

One day, Louie Synic brought a coconut to school. I had never seen one before. Louie was fifteen at that time. He gave me a chunk of it and told me to be sure and chew it really well or I'd turn into a monkey. I think I chewed that damned stuff until it was mush, before I swallowed it.

Soon as it was warm enough we would go to school bare footed. We stayed bare foot until the frost came in the fall. The teacher would have a wash basin and a pail of water handy where we could wash our feet, especially on rainy days when the roads would be muddy.

The clothes we wore were something else!!! We must have looked like a perpetual Halloween parade. Our winter clothing started with long underwear, made of wool and really itchy. We called them "woolie-boogers." They had a button up flap in the seat, so we wouldn't have to get undressed when nature called. Over these we wore long, brown cotton or woolen stockings that came up over our knees and were held up by rolling them over garters. Our shoes were brown high-top brogans, which laced up over our ankles. Everything we wore was hand-me-downs from older siblings or neighbors. Pa had a shoe last and all the stuff to re-sole and repair our shoes. When the bottoms would get holes, he would re-sole them. It was really neat watching him measure the leather and cut it, then nail it on to the shoes. Sometimes the nails stuck up through the soles, so we stuck newspaper in the bottom so our feet wouldn't get sore.

The first new article of clothing, besides my little shoes, was a white taffeta dress that Ma bought for me when I graduated from eighth grade, when I was twelve years old.

That was after we moved to Lee Center.

I thought I had died and gone to heaven! I was so proud of that dress. It crackled and rustled when I moved and had a lot of ruffles on it. I can imagine how *stunning* I must have been with that beautiful white dress and the long brown stockings and clod-hoppers on. But all that I noticed was the brand new dress.

Janie Pratt and I were the youngest girls in school when I started. Her brother, Sonny was a year older than I was, but our birthdays were on the same day. He vowed that he was going to marry me when we grew up. What a fickle boy he turned out to be!

One morning we were surprised in the classroom when the door burst open and a huge Hungarian man, with a gray drooping moustache, kinda like a big, fat walrus, flew into the room, pulling a reluctant boy and girl in each hand. They were the new neighbors. Esther Nemo had a mop of the blondest, curliest hair that we had ever seen. Frankie, her brother, was a year or two years older than Esther and his hair was dark and straight. They were the most nervous pair of kids I'd seen. Neither of them had ever been to school before and they didn't know what to expect. We soon made friends with them and it wasn't long before they felt right at home. The teacher would ask us what we had for breakfast that morning, to see if we were being fed properly, and how we would laugh when the Nemo kids would say "Prune-zoop." We had never heard of it. They also had blood sausage for their lunch.

I was nine years old when we moved from Fish Creek School in Taberg to the Union Free School in Lee Center. I took fifth and sixth grades together, (my teacher was Mrs. Minnie Mudge), and the seventh and eights grades together, so I was able to graduate at barely twelve years old. My seventh and eighth grade teacher was Mrs. Irene Robinson.

Then it was on to Junior High school in Rome, NY. We rode the bus to high school.

There were really some characters among the school students. The boys would get there early and put polly-wogs in the drinking water bottle. They would loosen the bolts in Mrs. Mudge's swivel chair, so when she came in and went to her seat, the chair would fly into a zillion pieces and the teacher ended up on the floor. She was well endowed in the behind, I think that saved her from getting hurt when she spun around or fell.

I don't know what Raymond Corr did to aggravate Mrs. Mudge, but one day she made him get under her desk. The first thing he did was reach his hand into her desk drawer from the back and fish out her lunch and ate it. He was a chubby teenager and tried to crawl out from under the desk, he got his head out, but the rest of him was stuck. Every time he would move she would kick him in the butt. It was so funny, but the class didn't dare laugh. I think that Raymond behaved himself after that.

In the middle of a Saluting of the Flag, before classes started, every once in awhile one of the smart-aleck boys would waltz out from the store room, with the human skeleton kept there for science class. That would get the whole class howling! It wasn't at all unusual for the kids in lower grades on the first floor to see things coming down on string or ropes from above. Shoes, boots, caps, or funny drawings, you name it, they thought of it. Lots of funny memories, but it drove the teachers looney.

High school and riding the school bus

We had to walk a mile or so to Lee Center to catch the school bus. A family named Siegfried lived near the bus stop. They had a big family too and several of their kids rode the bus. On cold days Mrs. Siegfried would let us in their house until the bus came.

Harold Payne was the bus driver. In the winter, sometimes the snow storms were so bad that he couldn't get to Rome to pick us up until late at night. He would follow the snow plows in to the school. While we were waiting for the bus to show up we would get into the auditorium and play on the piano and dance around like a bunch of hill-billy idiots that we were.

Some of the bigger boys would force the door to the kitchen, where the home making class learned to cook. We would be hungry and ate everything we could get our mitts on. I don't remember us getting into trouble for that.

There were some bullies on the bus. Sometimes they would get "Hy" Payne, the driver, and put him in the back of the bus and they would drive it, helter skelter. I don't know how he would get away from them, but I remember him kicking them out the back door and making them walk home. That was Clyde Corr and Darryl Moratt who usually thought up those escapades. They were worse than most kids are these days.

HARVEST TIME

Harvest time was a wonderful time. The farmers in the area helped each other get their haying in, silo filled with ensilage, and other chores that took a lot of time and effort. The hay had to be mowed and dried in the field. My brother, Buck, would let me ride on the rake when he drove the horse, and I would rake the hay up in rows. When it had dried enough to be put in the hay mow of the barn, everyone pitched in with their pitch forks and made the rows of hay into mounds that I thought looked like Indian teepees. One of the men would go up and down the rows of hay with the team of horses and hay wagon and a pair of men on each side would pitch the hay onto the wagon. My father would let us smaller kids ride on the hay wagon and keep the hay distributed evenly. When it was loaded it looked like a big lumbering elephant coming through the fields. We would ride home atop the mounds of hay laughing like idiots!

When the hay would get to the barn, they would unhitch the team of horses, give them water and let them rest. There was a big beam in the roof of the barn that ran the length of the hay mow. A rope and pulley was fastened to it, which would lift the hay fork up with bundles of hay from the wagon. The team of horses pulled the rope that guided and lifted the hay fork. Usually a couple of adults and some kids would be up in the mow with pitch forks to scatter the hay evenly when it was dropped from the fork. It was hotter than an oven in the hay mow. I didn't like that job. But I did like to jump in the hay afterwards.

My father usually had a big pail or jug of oatmeal water to quench their thirst. He would put in a couple of hands full of raw oats in the pail and fill it with water from the spring, then he would start out for the fields. I guess it worked. It was good anyhow. Sometimes we would have vinegar, sugar and water drink for a thirst quencher. It tasted a lot like cider. We loved that too.

The corn was picked (not by me, I couldn't stand to touch or even listen to corn husks) and put in cribs to dry. It was a lot of hard, back breaking work for everyone.

I remember my mother making cakes, pies and puddings, days in advance to get ready for the big dinners. It was almost like Thanksgiving time. The smaller kids would pick black berries and blue berries for pies. We also picked apples for pies and apple sauce. The pumpkins from our garden were made into pies also.

Our harvest dinners usually consisted of mashed potatoes, heaps and heaps of them and gravy, baked beans, sliced tomatoes, squash and all kinds of vegetables, fresh from our garden. There was also homemade bread and butter, buttermilk, lemonade, coffee and tea. Any hen that wasn't laying eggs up to her potential and a few of the roosters, got their heads lopped off and ended up as platters of fried chicken or chicken'n-dumplin's (my favorite)! My mother would move our huge dining table, with its many leaves, out onto the lawn, where everyone could sit and eat.

Before my father got his "Allis-Chalmers" tractor, all of the work was done with the help of the horses. Our neighbor, Bill Corr, supplied the horse power and sometimes my brother-in-law, Wonder Hayes, would come down with his team and wagon loaded down with my sister Mickey and their group of youngsters. My father had a real old STAR car, he took the tires off the wheels, put it up on blocks, and used the wheels with canvas belts on them (powered by the engine) to carry the ensilage up to the silos.

The little kids, me, included, climbed up in the silos to tramp the ensilage down. That was really a blast! I think I turned out to be one of the best ensilage stompers around!

After our work of the day was done, we would grab a bar of soap, washrag and towel, and who ever had a car would load us up and drive out to Delta Lake for a bath and swim. Those were good days!

Remsen, N.Y. 1923
Edwin Wood holding Tyke. Jack, Tom and Buck.

HARVEST TIME

THE WILDCAT

When we moved to the Bill Dust farm and Pa started buying cows and building up his dairy, it was Mary's and my chore to take a half gallon of milk to the neighbors who had moved into our old place, the Charlie Lemon house down the road. The first people who moved in there was a couple, Mr. and Mrs. Castro, and their little boy who was about three years old at the time. Mrs. Castro was very sick at the time. I don't know what happened to them. After they moved away the Heaney family moved in. There was Bob and Charlotte and their children, Lansing, Glenwood and Mary Jane. There was a creek across the road from our place that flooded in the winter and made a great place for ice skating and sliding on the ice from our home all the way to Lee Center.

Mary and I would slide on the ice when we delivered the milk if it was a bright night with the moon out. One night, when we were on our way back home, we heard the most terrible screaming we had ever heard. It really sounded like a woman screaming. It sent chills and goose bumps up my spine.

Mary said "Wild cat!" and we began to run and slip and slide on the ice. The faster we would run the closer the screaming got to us. When we got close to home, I don't remember if we went over or through the barbed wire fence, we were running so fast. I was so out of breath and could feel my lungs burning from inhaling the cold air and running so fast. Ma said that it was a "Bobcat" and must have been stalking us. I don't remember if anyone shot it or not. But we were very careful and stayed on the road where the houses were from then on when we made our milk delivery.

(Charlotte Heaney's niece, Jeannette Austin from Rome, visited her one summer and met my brother Buck. It must have been love at first sight, as they went together from then on and eventually got married in 1944).

Speaking of the wild cat, Tyke just missed being attacked when he was working for a couple in Lee Valley. He said it leaped at him when he was pumping water from the outside pump to carry in the house. I think the old man shot that one. I don't remember who the folks were that he worked for at the time, but I remember him telling us that the man and wife weren't speaking to each other. They would communicate through Tyke. All three would be in the room and she would tell him what to tell the old man or vice versa. He thought they were really nutty. I don't think he worked for them for very long. I do remember going over to Lee Valley to see him when he worked there. The thing that I liked was a curved, stone bridge across a creek, on the way. I had never seen one like it before; I liked to climb down by the creek and just watch and listen to the water flowing over and around the rocks and cat tails.

WORLD WAR II

We started hearing about a coming war in 1936. Franklin Delano Roosevelt was the President of the United States at the time. In fact, he was the only president in my lifetime. I thought he was there forever. There were forty-eight stars on the U.S. flag. Winston Churchill was Prime Minister of England, Charles DeGaulle of France, Adolph Hitler was dictator of Germany, Benito Mussollini dictator of Italy and Hiro Hito of Japan.

The whole town was upset over it. Hitler's and Japan's armies were invading countries and Mussolini from Italy joined Hitler. My brother Buck was working in the canning factory when he felt the "urge" to defend our country. Tyke was out in the garden plowing. Buck and a friend of his, LaVere Fox, came to tell Tyke of their decision to "join up." Tyke didn't hesitate a bit, he left the horse and plow standing in the garden and off they went. Tyke wasn't old enough to join-up yet so the recruiter came to the house to get the folks to sign for him.

That old horse stood in the garden for a long time, until someone realized that Tyke was gone.

Tom was working at the Oneida Silverware factory in Oneida, NY. He was drafted shortly after Buck and Tyke's escapade. I think it was at least six months later that Jack was inducted into the Army Air Force.

Buck, Tyke and LaVere joined the Infantry. Tom was in the Army Engineers, and worked on the Alcan (Alaskan) highway.

When they went overseas, Pa got a huge map and stuck it up on the dining room wall. It took up most of the wall it was so big. Whenever they would hear from the boys, they would mark where they were on the map with thumb tacks.

Everyone with sons in the service had stars hung in their windows. When a soldier was killed in action, they were gold stars. There were quite a few "Gold Star Mothers" in Lee Center.

My brother Buck (Killed in Germany) and Chet Sczwyck were the first fatalities from Lee Center. Darryl Moratt was "missing in action" and to this day no one knows what happened to him. My brother Tyke was shot by the Japanese in Burma. He spent a long time in the Reed Veterans hospital in Utica. I know there were several others who lost their lives from our area, but I don't remember their names.

My father was one of the wardens in our area. He made sure that everyone had their windows covered or the lights extinguished when there were black outs so the enemy couldn't see our villages if they flew over. I don't believe that there were any enemy events. I remember having nightmares of the Japs getting us.

UNCLE STILL

Now, to "Uncle Still–The Rattling Cannon Ball." No one ever knew when he would turn up. He would just show up out of the blue on his bicycle. He would ride it all the way to New York from Wisconsin. He was tall and skinny with a shock of dark hair. He had a "hawk-nose," which Ma said was from falling in the gutter when he was cleaning the barn once. He didn't have much common sense either.

We never knew where he had been or why he chose to visit us. Ma always had a bed and spare food for him. I don't remember him ever having a job. I think he went from place to place and mooched as long as he could.

He was a "gassy" old coot too. When the family would retire for the night, we'd wait to hear the booms coming from Still's room. Especially if we had beans for supper that night, he could be heard all over the house.

The first "explosion" from his room would get one or two of the kids giggling, and before long we were in stitches. Guessing how long it would be before the next "blast off." I think if his butt was packed with bullets and he was fed a mess of beans, all they would have to do was point him at the enemy and he would win the war single handed ! That's how he got the name

"Rattling Cannonball!"

When he had decided that he had worn out his welcome, off he'd go. He lived with a lot of people around the Lee Center area. Don't know if he ever did any work or not. He finally married a wealthy woman, Evangeline Spargo, from Rome, NY. Her father was one of the owners of The Spargo Wire Mills in Rome. After her father, Tom Spargo died, Stillman talked Evangeline into selling their lovely home on Liberty Street in Rome and buying a forty acre farm in the country, even though he knew nothing about farming. They eventually lost the farm and all of their money and ended up living in a remodeled "chicken house" on my parents' farm. Destitute!

Update: Jane Pratt and I have been friends for eighty plus years. She lives in Lee Center, NY now. She and Howard VanEtten have been married over fifty years. They raised their family and now have grand and great-grandchildren. The last time I visited with her, Lizzie Lower was living with them. Jane gave her a home until her death several years ago.

Update: Jane phoned me for Christmas on Dec. 22, 2004. She and Howard loved my "memory" stories. She corrected me on what the Indian Woman, who lived with the Clarks name was. It was Nellie Waters. Jane kept in touch with her and the Clarks after they moved to Rome and she cared for Nellie in her home for the rest of Nellie's life. Jane also reminded me about Boyd's Hill. She said when she went back there to look around, it wasn't nearly as big as we thought it was and it wasn't as far away from our house as we thought either. I find that the things we remembered as kids, were much smaller as we grew up.

****

THE GREAT DEPRESSION

I really didn't know much about a depression or even what it was. All I remember was moving around a lot and never having enough to eat.

When we moved from Fish Creek in Taberg to Lee Center, NY, it seemed like everybody was in the same boat, except those who could find jobs or already had work. These people included the teachers, store owners, drug stores, mail men etc.

My first year in the Lee Center Free School, the teacher asked each student to bring a can of food of some sort for the "poor box" which was to go to the poorest family in the area.

I don't know what my siblings took, but Ma gave me a can of canned milk to take. I felt so proud being able to contribute to the "Poorest

Family." I thought it must be someone really, really poor.

Imagine my surprise on the day before Thanksgiving to see a car pull into our yard. It was Elmer Liebe, from Liebe's grocery store in Lee Center, driving his father's car.

When Ma came to the door, he started bringing in baskets and packages, including turkey with all the trimmings and stuff to make a wonderful Thanksgiving dinner. Ma was so happy and couldn't thank him enough.

Well! Elmer Liebe went to the same school that I did. I was never so embarrassed in my life when I found out that WE were the "Poorest People" in the area. I couldn't hold my head up at school or around town. That is when I realized that we were poor!

(Liebe's store was catty-corner from Hartson's. Liebe's also had a gas station in front of the store, where everybody bought their gas. There was also a Red and White store on Main Street across the street from the Protestant Church. I don't know how such a small town kept all of these stores in business.)

We went to Hartson's grocery store, which was a combination mercantile, grocery, Post office and a meeting place, where the old men would sit around the pot belly stove and swap stories and spit in the spittoons during winter. It was a big store, with wooden floors that were stained and worn with years of use. It had a mixture of aromas, from kerosene for lamps and stoves, shoes and leather and wearing apparel, spices, food and a big wooden pickle barrel, and just about everything but the kitchen sink. You could probably find that too, if you had time to look through all the goods they had. The front porch was the length of the whole store and us kids used to like to "hang out" (as the kids say today) there.

I remember the "Relief" stores that gave food and clothing to people who were without the necessities of life. A lot like the food banks that we have today. It was items that couldn't be sold anyhow. The flour was full of mouse droppings and there were worms in the rice and cereal. I remember when we made bread we had to sift the mouse droppings out of the flour. A kid never forgets those things!

I also went to the Methodist church in Lee Center where I would sing on Sunday along with everyone else. Mrs. Hartson would tell me to keep quiet as my voice was too loud and I couldn't sing. I believe that is the last time I went to that church except for the youth programs they had on Sunday nights. I still went to Sunday school. I would bring two pennies, one for God and one for me to get a piece of candy at Clyde Felshaw's drug store on the way home. (The Felshaw's store was almost across the street from the Hartsons.

They kept their store spotless; they sold drugs, greeting cards, and of course candy. They had a daughter, Shirley and were all very nice people.)

I do think that God was supposed to get both pennies, but Satan must have been pushing me to get candy too. I usually got two sassafras "barrels" for a penny.

THE GREAT DEPRESSION

PA'S BLACKSMITH SHOP

Pa's blacksmith shop was in one of the sheds behind the house. I think he must have carted that big iron anvil around with him wherever he went. He also had a forge and all the accouterments that went with it. There was a foot pedal to blow the air into the forge. I used to like doing that, made me feel like a "big shot" when I would help him. He burned coal in the forge. I liked to see the coal turn red and when it was hot enough he would put a piece of metal in it with a long pair of tongs which looked like a long handled pliers to me. The metal would stay in the coals until it was white hot, and then he would lay it on the anvil and hammer it with his big hammer, turning and twisting it, dunking it in cold water and redoing the process over and over until he got the shape that he wanted. He could make just about anything that he needed for repairing his car, tractor and equipment. He even made ma a huge butcher knife out of a big file that he had on hand.

There was also a grinding wheel contraption. It had a seat like a bicycle and pedals; the front "wheel" was the grindstone. It sat in what looked like half of an old tire that was filled with water. He would let me pedal it while he sharpened whatever needed it on the grindstone. He later had it electrified and everything ran at the touch of a switch. He even had an electric hammermill that he ground his corn and food for the animals with. I remember one day he dropped one of his wrenches in it when it was going and it was pulverized. I often wonder if the younger kids had as much fun "helping" him out in the shop as I did.

BARN DANCING

When I was a teenager, Mick and Wonder (My sister Mickey) would take me with them to "Crowfoots" barn. I believe it was on Stokes Hill.

They had local players, with guitar, banjo, piano and "whatever" who played music and called out the dances. We did the square dance and polkas. There were rows of benches along the wall and blocks of hay to sit on for the old folks, children and wall flowers. They also had a refreshment stand to buy sodas, candy and snacks.

They would have the barn floor swept clean and would sprinkle saw dust or sand on it to make it danceable and slippery. That was a lot of fun.

The smart-aleck guys had bottles of "hootch"

in their cars and they and their gals would go out between dances and slug a few down. By the end of night they were feeling no pain and could have danced all night.

WOODMAN'S HALL

The first moving picture that I ever saw was held at Woodman's Hall in Lee Center; right on the corner of Liebe's grocery store and Main Street. It was *The Shoemaker and The Elves*. I was fascinated and will never forget it.

They would have something for the local kids to go to about once a month.

When I grew older, Ma would walk down there from our house with us kids to dances etc. I don't remember if they had a band or a juke box. I always danced with the girls. No *boys* for me!

Years later it was remodeled into the "Lee Center Inn." My sister Mickey was a waitress there. They had their special "Fish Fry" on Fridays. There was also a bar and dance floor.

My parents had their fiftieth wedding

anniversary there in 1964. Most of the townsfolk attended and all eleven of their children were there. Over 300 people attended in all.

THE CHEESE FACTORY

On Main Street in Lee Center, going toward Stokes, there was an old cheese factory. Gratt Lemon's future wife's family owned and operated it. (In fact the Stevens' Family owned it years before that, before they moved to Oneida, NY. Dorothy Stevens was Uncle Tom's future wife.)

Anyhow, there was a big pond by the factory with a big rock in it. The local kids used to go swimming there. We would get up on the big rock and use it for a diving board. The stream ran under a bridge, it wasn't deep there and we would sit under there to get out of the hot sun. And to "skip school" if it was a hot day.

THE CHEESE FACTORY

FISH CREEK

When we lived in Fish Creek, across from the Suiter's place, Belle was still living at home with us. The older kids would go swimming at the Fish Creek Bridge. It seemed like a long ways to me, as they would walk down to Clarks, and turn left toward Taberg. Anyone going to Taberg had to cross it.

Eddie and I would find the "bath tubs" in the rocks, caused from the flooding, fast waters, and would play in them. We also found shale rocks with the imprint of fish, leaves (mostly ferns) and small insects imbedded in them. I wonder sometimes if rocks with those imprints are still there as they would be collector items today.

Sometimes, after a big rain and the river

flooded, there would be big fish caught in the "bath tubs." The older kids could catch them in their hands. I thought they were trout, but Tom has corrected me, he said they were cat-fish or "suckers." When they caught some Ma would cook them for supper. They were good, but had a lot of bones that we had to be careful of.

One day, when the older kids had gone swimming there by themselves, Buck got pulled down by the whirlpool under the bridge. I think the water was a lot deeper then. Anyhow, Belle, who was afraid of nothing, pinched her nose shut with one hand and walked along the bottom of the river and grabbed buck's head of thick, red hair and pulled him out. One of the kids ran home and told Ma that Buck had drowned. They met her on the road when they were bringing him home, no worse for wear.

Belle was the daredevil of the family. She also had a wonderful singing voice and we loved it when she sang.

Ma would tell of Belle, Maggie and Mickey when they were little and lived in Remsen, and Pa worked for Brate Fuller. The "Rattling Cannon Ball" must have lived there too. Belle used to get in a milk can; Maggie and Mickey would put the lid on it, then call "Still." Belle would call him and he would look all over for her and could never find her. In the winter they would dig a big deep hole in the snow and cover Belle, and pack it down on her. They drove Still almost crazy trying to find her. He would walk all over her "grave," and she would keep calling him, but to no avail.

The folks also told of a bull in a pasture near there, he was coming after the kids while they were going across lots. Belle stared the bull down and chased it clear across the field.

I don't remember much of the older girls, except that I slept with Belle and Mary when we lived at the old house across from Merritt Pratt's place. We didn't get much sleep in the winter, as the house was so cold and we didn't have many bed covers. They used their coats as covers at night for extra warmth. The one in the middle would get hot and change places with one of the "outsiders" so they could get warm too. That went on all night, so we were usually tired during the day.

Belle and Mickey had to quit school when they were sixteen and go out to work and give their money for the home. I don't remember where Mickey worked, but I know that Belle worked for Grace Fye, taking care of her houseful of kids. She lived up in Northern New York someplace. Belle said that Grace Fye dressed like a man, chewed tobacco, and worked like a man. But she was always having more kids, so she wasn't "Queer."

I think Maggie was working for Grace when

she met Louie Mulvaney and went up to Camden to live with him and work on his farm. She took Dickie along with her. I sure did miss him when she took him away from home. She and Louie would bring him back home when he needed a haircut. He had very curly, blonde hair and it would grow so long, he looked like a cute little girl. In fact, he and Esther could have passed for twins. Only Dick's hair was curly and Esther's was straight as a pin.

That is about all I can remember of the older girls.

FISH CREEK

MEMORIES OF GROWING UP

Yes, I was nicknamed "Hayseed" by Belle and Mickey's boyfriends. They said that was the very name for me, as that is what I looked like. A "country bumpkin." The name stuck, especially in my very young years.

MEMORIES OF GROWING UP

THE GAMES WE PLAYED

We didn't have "real games." In fact, we didn't even know there were such things. We used to stomp on tin cans so they would fit our feet, and go clopping around, pretending we were horses. Even did the snorting and neighing bit. We had the iron hoops from the wagon wheels and wheelbarrows. We could spend most of an afternoon rolling them up and down the road. Of course, we had the usual games of "Hide and Seek"; "Hop Scotch"; "Tag"; "Ollie-Ollie Oxen Free" trying to get one of the boys' homemade balls over the roof of the house. In the evening we spent our time catching fireflies and seeing how many we could get in a fruit jar. We did manage to keep ourselves entertained. It was a fun time.

THE GAMES WE PLAYED

GETTING IN MA AND PA'S BED

I remember when I was little and would get sick, Ma would let me get in their bed. That was as special treat. It still had the comforting, warm, smell of my parents. I would have to stick out my tongue, and if it had a white coating, I was *sick*!

Ma would make some toast and tea. She would lift the lid off the wood stove and toast the bread over the wood flames. I don't think I have ever tasted such "good" toast since then. If there were any eggs, she would poach one for me. She would fluff the pillows and have me sit up, and bring me this "special" treat in bed.

It made me feel special, and it wasn't long until I was *better* and up and around. This is one of my best memories from growing up. I suppose she did this for the other kids too, because I wasn't coddled or treated any better than the rest.

WHEN LLOYD WAS BORN

We never noticed when Ma was pregnant. She always looked that way and little kids didn't notice things like that in those days. Besides, the "stork" brought the babies.

Anyhow, I remember it being days that Ma was gone. (She was in the hospital in Rome having her next to last baby). When Pa brought her back home, she had a little baby boy with her. And he was really little! The nurses at the hospital named him "Peanuts." As I grew older and knew more about that stuff, I find that Ma had a very hard time birthing him. She almost died. He was named after David Lloyd George, of Wales.

As he grew, and started to crawl around the house; he was a beautiful little boy. Had a head full of curly, corn silk colored hair. I used to wrap his hair around a pencil and make nice curls. It must have been my job to take care of him and I enjoyed it. He could do no wrong in my eyes. We all called him Lloydie Boy!

(I don't remember much about Esther at that time, she must have been Mary's job. "Poor Esther!")

One day, after us older kids scoured the fields and hills for wild strawberries, (The wild ones were really small then, they took a long time to find and pick. And an even longer time to hull and clean them) Ma made strawberry jam (on the wood stove, which heated the house more on a hot, humid, day) and put it on the lower shelf of the pantry, so the cool air from the window wouldn't break the jars. She had to walk to Lee Center to get some more sugar and she told me to watch Lloydie Boy so he wouldn't get into it. (We were living in The Charlie Lemon place in

Lee Center at this time.)

I was busy washing dishes and looking at myself in the tin mirror above the sink when

things got too quiet around the kitchen and I noticed that Lloyd was missing.

He was in the pantry, up to his elbow in a quart jar of jam. His face was covered in jam and I thought he looked so cute. Ma came home with the sugar and I called her into the pantry to take a look. Well! She took a look alright and was as mad as a hornet. She grabbed the first thing she could find, being my luck it was the broom, and she beat the pee-waddin' out of me with the broom handle. After all of her hard work it wasn't a bit funny to her.

It was a year or so after Lloyd's birth that she lost another child. She was in the hospital a very long time, that time. She had to have her legs elevated and I remember her saying that she had to eat chopped, raw liver, to build her blood up.

WHEN LLOYD WAS BORN

WHEN PA SMELLED SMOKE

Pa told the story of seeing puffs of smoke coming from behind the spring house out in the pasture, where he kept the milk during the night to keep it cold, so he could take it to the milk factory in West Branch in the morning. That water was really cold, like ice.

He went across the creek and pasture to the spring house and peeked around it. There were my nephews, Mike, Davie and my brother Lloyd. They had swiped some of Pa's cigars and were having a dandy old time puffing away. They had a bag of onions with them to chew on afterwards, so you couldn't smell the smoke on them. Pa told them if they wanted to smoke to go ahead and finish their cigars. He stood there until the kids finished them or had turned green and were so sick they could hardly stand up to walk to the house. That's one lesson they learned from Gramps.

"LLOYDIE-BOY" AND THE CIDER BARREL

The kids would pick apples from the orchard and Pa took them to the flour mill in West Branch, where there was a cider press and the apples were given a water bath and pressed into cider, usually a barrel. Pa would also take his cans of milk there to be picked up by the milk factories.

Lloyd was four or five when this happened. It was spring and Pa couldn't find him anyplace, he had everyone looking for him. Pa decided to look in the cellar, as a last resort. There was "Lloydie-Boy," stretched out on the floor dead to the world! He had found a small siphon hose and had it inserted in a barrel of cider and had sucked up the dregs from the barrel. He was drunk as a skunk! The cider had turned "hard" over the winter and was unfit to drink. He was a pretty sick boy for awhile. I often wonder if he had a hang-over at that young age.

(I have heard from Lloyd and Mike since I wrote this that Mike was in on it too!)

THERE AIN'T NO SANTA, FOOL!

I still believed in Santa Clause when I was ten years old. I don't know why, as we never got any presents. But there was always peanut brittle and an orange in our stockings on Christmas morning. So there just "had to be."

In 1936, I had written a letter to the Editor of the *Rome Daily Sentinel* in Rome, NY for a contest of "Why I Believe in Santa," and won two tickets to a Christmas movie in Rome. I don't remember just what I wrote, but I was on cloud nine.

My little niece, Clara L. Hayes, was six months old that December. She was the sweetest baby. Mick and Wonder would bring her down home often and would always let me hold and play with her. I'd hold her up on the table and sing la-la-la to her and she would laugh and jig.

She came down with pneumonia just before Christmas, and as penicillin had not been discovered yet, it was a fatal illness. She died shortly before Christmas. I forgot about going to the show or anything as it was a very sad time that year. We were still living at Charlie Lemon's place at that time.

After we moved to the Bill Dust farm, I still half believed and hoped he was real, so I hung my stocking up with Eddie, Esther and Lloyd, before climbing "the wooden hill" to our beds.

Mary was helping Ma dress out chickens that evening, to sell to some of Ma's "clients" in Rome, who always bought their chickens and eggs from her. It was Christmas day, but Pa and Ma went to Rome early in the morning and took the chickens to the people who had ordered them, also to make Christmas dinner for us.

When I hung my stocking, she looked at me

with disgust. "There ain't no Santa, you dang fool," she hissed at me. The next morning when we came down stairs, my stocking was full, along with the rest of the kids. I made a face at Mary and said gleefully, "See, there is too a Santa!" She watched me with a smirk on her face while I tore into my package. When I opened it what fell out but a chicken head and guts. Mary was doubled over in laughter. That was the end of Santa and fairy tales for me.

THERE AIN'T NO SANTA, FOOL!

TYKES "LOVE LETTERS"

I think that Tyke was the "free-soul" in our family. He came and went as he pleased saying it was no use asking if he could go places, as the folks would only say no. So he would go, and take his punishment when he got home.

Whenever he came home from one of his escapades, or from his job at the Canning factory, or working for an old couple in Lee Valley, we could hear him a mile or so away. We could hear him singing and yodeling, when he came around the bend in the road, which was a good long walk from home. Ma would say, "Tyke's coming down the road"!

When I was in grade school in Lee Center, Tyke was in high school in Rome. He must have made an impression on the girls, as they would send him "mash notes." One girl in particular, and I'll never forget her name if I live to be 100, Tyke made sure of that, was Yolanda T. He had a pack of love letters stashed away under his mattress, and I found them! Hee, hee, hee!

My best girlfriends in Lee Center were Cora and Milly Beckley, Sarah Alder and Florence and Leone MacDonald. They came to visit me one day and we were in the living room gabbing. I was telling them about "The Letters" and they wanted to hear them too. So I went upstairs and got them and was in the process of reading them to the girls and having a blast, giggling and laughing, when Tyke came in and caught me. He was mad and ready to kill! I could almost see my whole life passing before my eyes! He grabbed them out of my hand and with one good punch, knocked me clear across the room. He must have gave up on Yolanda after that, as he never received notes from her anymore. So Mary wasn't the only one with a mean streak in the family, I'll have to confess that I was as bad as the rest.

TYKES "LOVE LETTERS"

OUR CHRISTMAS TREE

Jack always made sure we had a Christmas tree. Ma didn't want the mess of putting one up and decorating it, and as us kids were older, we didn't need one, Ma said. But Jack would go up in the woods behind the farm and cut a good big one down. The top would almost touch the ceiling. He would cut tin cans into strips with the tin snips, wrap them around a pencil and make icicles. Then he would take crepe paper and cut it into strips and let us kids paste them into circles which he would make into chains and hang on the tree. Ma had some candle holders in the shape of birds that were clipped on the tree. They burned real candles too. Jack would dig out all the ornaments to trim the tree. Some were really old that Ma had kept over the years.

Anyhow, we had a tree. And it was pretty! Ma would let Jack light the candles for a little while on Christmas Eve, then blow them right out so the tree wouldn't catch on fire. Of course we younger kids thought it was magic.

Jack also used to make paper dolls for me and Esther. He would draw and color them and cut them out, then make the clothes for them. They were complete with the tabs on so we could dress the dolls. He also made us spool knitters. He took Ma's "wooden" thread spools and pounded four nails on the top. We would attach yarn to the nails, with the tail end hanging through the hole. Then we would slip the yarn over the nails, pull on the tail and it wasn't long before we had a long woven braid. When it was long enough, we rolled it up and sewed it together for pot holders etc. He made "tractors" for Eddie and Lloyd. He would take one of Ma's wooden spools and cut Vs along the flat ends. Then he would put a rubber band through the hole and attach match sticks to the end and wind the rubber band up. When it was let go it would crawl across the floor. I think he was much more soft-hearted than the rest of the boys. I guess he was the clever one.

OUR CHRISTMAS TREE

"TWM THE TERRIBLE"

When Tom was born he was Pa's pride and joy. After having three daughters he was delighted when Tom came along. He was called "Twm" as that is how it was pronounced in Welsh. He was the torturer of the family. I remember when I was little and Ma and Pa would go someplace, I would follow their car down the road like a puppy dog, screaming to go with them. Sometimes they would stop and take me along. But I remember the days that they didn't!

As soon as the folks were gone, Twm would get me on the floor and sit on me, with his knees on my arms so I couldn't move; hold a pillow over my face until I could hardly breathe. He thought that was fun, watching me scream and almost turn blue. He would also lock me in the dark closet and listen to me howl. I don't know what kind of punishment he would mete out to the rest of the kids, but I do remember mine. He'd say if I told Ma and Pa about it, I would only get it worse the next time. So I didn't dare tell. I think he really "ruled the roost" with the other kids too. And to think that he grew up to be one of the best "Church goers" in the family. Thank God for that! I thought he'd turn out to be an axe murderer or something like that, for sure. Buck, Jack and Tyke followed Twm in rapid succession, but they were never as close to Pa as Twm.

TOM'S MEMORIES

Tom and I reminisce about our childhood, especially now in our later years, when we get together. He is eight years older than I am, so I guess he knows what he's talking about!

This is from Tom's "memory bank."

He said Pa and Ma were buying the house on Thomas Street just outside of Rome, NY, across the road from the gravel pit. I think it was (might still be) The Sullivan Gravel Pit. I was a baby when we moved there and Eddie was born there.

He said Pa had a steady job, so they had money in the bank, insurance policies on the kids etc. Then the depression happened! The Stock Market crashed and hundreds of people lost their jobs, Pa included. The bank foreclosed on their home loan; took his money he had in the bank, cancelled the insurance policies etc. The family was put out in the street with just the clothes on their backs and what they could carry from the house. Ma had a big vegetable garden, but they weren't even allowed to take any of it.

Tom said an old couple by the name of Dealy, took the whole family of ten kids and Pa and Ma in to live with them. I do remember "Grandma and Grandpa Dealy" as we called them, but just by their names. I don't remember much about living with them or how long we lived with them, but Tom said our family was shuffled around from place to place. My first real memories were of living in the Perkoski place across from the Suiters, in Fish Creek.

Tom tells of when we lived in the house across from Merritt Pratt's, a man by the name of Louie Lake and his sister from somewhere up North would come to visit us. They found out about our family from a friend of theirs, an Indian woman who visited the Clarks. As I mentioned before, her name was Nellie Waters.

Louie Lake was searching for a bride for his father. He was very interested in Belle, as she was young and "pure." He was trying to make a marriage transaction with Pa. (Fathers must have still been making arrangements for their daughters at that time.) But Belle would have none of that. She wasn't going to marry any "Old Goat." I didn't know the reason they came to visit our family, I thought they were family friends. I do know they used to bring bushels of the biggest apples that we had ever seen. Tom remembers them as being humongous too. We came to the conclusion that they must have been Northern Spy Apples.

Tom also remembers having to quit school when he was sixteen to go to work with Pa, to make more money for the family. I think Pa had a WPA job working on the Barge Canal in Rome,

NY widening the canal and replacing the paths along the canal, where horses were used to tow the barges. They had new barges with engines and didn't need the horses anymore.

While Pa was working, he was hauling loads of rocks and dirt in a wheelbarrow, and then something happened to his back and he was completely paralyzed. He was unable to move or talk and all he could move was his eyes. He was in the County Hospital in Rome for quite awhile. Pa remembered that the nurses used to cram pills in his mouth and didn't even give him water to swallow them with. One day he ended up in the hospital morgue, covered with a sheet. He knew everything that was going on, but couldn't respond to anything. He made himself move his eyes when the sheet was removed from him. Thank God! Or that probably would have been the end of the story.

Ma had someone bring him home from the

hospital and she took care of him herself. She alternated putting hot and cold packs on him. When it was warm outside she would have someone take him down to fish creek, along with her laundry and wash tubs. She and the older kids would build a fire on the beach to boil the clothes then she and the older girls would rinse them in the creek, and hang them on the bushes along the creek to dry.

She would put Pa in the water and make him move his arms and legs. All I remember about it is the big pot of homemade soup she would take, along with several loaves of homemade bread for our lunch. (I think she knew how to care for Pa as a result of her working as a nurse in the Old Soldier's Home in Wisconsin, where she was working when she met Pa.)

I do remember Pa creeping on the floor with Mary, Eddie and me. I also remember when he was able to sit up in the rocking chair and hold us little ones on his lap and sing and tell us stories of when he was a cowboy. I don't remember how long it took him to learn to walk and talk again. I know that he could, when we lived across from Merritt Pratt's, as we all used to walk down to the Clarks to visit and sing. He fully recovered in every way, except he didn't have the great strength that he used to have.

OUR RURAL MAILMAN

Our rural mailman was Floyd Schmitt "Smitty." He took his mailman oath to heart. He brought our mail, no matter the weather. When the roads were too muddy for a car, he would walk in with his high lace-up boots on. When the roads were blocked with snow, he would come on snow shoes. Sometimes it was late at night or on Sundays if it was too late. He would stop in for a hot cup of coffee and pass on some local gossip. But he always brought the mail, we could depend on that. When Pa and Ma got a letter we would all gather around, so they could read it to us. Letters were for the whole family in those days.

"Smitty's" route took him up on Capron Road where Mick and Wonder lived. He went there first. We didn't have telephones in those days, so Mickey and Leaty would send messages down to our house with him "for free," when they wanted us for something. The notes were usually from Leaty wanting me to come up and play with her.

The school in Lee Center let out a week or so before her school did, so I would go up and go to her school. I remember the Seldens who lived up the road from them and Winton "Wint" and Ginny Webster. They were really nice.

Sometimes I'd just take a notion to go up to Mick's and Ma would let me. I'd take the back road which was out of Lee Center a ways. It was a short-cut on a narrow dirt road. I'd stop and visit a couple of families along the way. Louie Fox and his mother lived on that road and if they were in the yard I'd chat with them awhile.

I liked to stop at the Webster's house. The mother and father were first cousins, their oldest son, George and youngest son Raymond, were "dim-witted," so everyone said because of cousins marrying. Winton "Wint" and Ginny were normal. We were friends for many years.

I liked to visit them mainly to hear the old folks talk. They used a lot of "old-timer" words, such as: They would greet me with, "Waaal Haller thar Sarey, come on in. How be ya? We's all well heer."

Or "We heer'd bout something or other. Yonder and yon and you go that-a-way or this-a-way." I was fascinated and could listen to them talk for hours.

On up the road to Mickey's, the thing Leaty and I liked to play with was an old car, without wheels, that was propped up on blocks. It did have a steering wheel though. Leaty and I would take turns "driving" that thing. I don't know how many hundreds of miles we drove.

We would make mud pies, and steal eggs out of the hen house to add to our "batter." I wonder how many innocent hens wound up on the dinner table for not laying eggs anymore.

Another old friend of mine was Alice Conover. Wonder's first wife was the sister of Ivy Conover, Alice's mother. I would go with Mick and Wonder when they would visit. Alice was several years younger than me. I loved to visit and listen to them talk. And I especially liked Alice's grandmother. I don't remember what she looked like but I do remember that she smoked a clay pipe! She would get settled in her chair, take the pipe out of her apron pocket and light it up. The first time I saw it my eyes almost popped out of my head. Holy cow! That old woman was smoking!

It was very embarrassing to Alice, but I thought it was "Cool" as the kids say today.

I used to go to the school playground; Alice lived right across from it. We would spin around on the merry-go-round. Her brother Louie was just about two or three years old and we would take him along. He called me Saddie and Alice Akkie.

She wanted me to play only with her, but I preferred to hang out with friends in my age bracket which didn't sit well with Alice and we had many arguments. We grew up without me killing her and we are still the best of friends to this day. What memories we hash over when we correspond!

OUR RURAL MAILMAN

GOIN' CROSS-LOTS TO SCHOOL

Sometimes when the bread wasn't ready to make sandwiches (our sandwiches were usually mayonnaise or mustard and bread) or there wasn't enough for all of us, I would come home from school at noontime. I would go cross-lots through the field. I would get home in half the time and get a hot meal.

One day, when I was going cross-lots, I saw a good sized chunk of "glass" by a stone wall. I thought there must have been a heck of a fire there at sometime or other to make glass melt like that. It was almost pure glass with a tinge of blue-green, like some of the old bottles back then. Anyhow, I took it home with me. Ma used it as a door-stop for years. I don't know whatever happened to it.

*(I saw some just like it in 2004 in Washington State. Some friends had several of them by their fish pond. There are also some in gem stores. He said it was a meteorite and worth a lot of money. I wonder if someone came along and knew what it was and admired it and Ma gave it to them? That would be like something she would do. If someone liked something that she had, she would give it to them.)

THE OLD WATERING TROUGH

I don't know if any of you remember the old, wooden, watering trough at the foot of Graves Hill; seems like it was there forever. I sometimes wonder if it is still there. It was going out of Lee Center toward Rome. There was a metal pipe coming out of the side of the hill, with fresh, cold, spring water flowing out of it. People passing through there would stop for a good cup of water. When there was a drought or someone was having problems with their well water, we would go there and get our milk cans full to take home. Eddie and I were wandering around there one day on our way to Lee Valley. If you turned right by the watering trough, that would take you to Lee Valley too. We decided to climb up on the hill to see what was there. There must have been an old town there at some time. We found a gravestone of a little girl, I don't remember the name on it, but we would often go up there and put flowers on the grave. We didn't find any signs of old houses or anything though. Across the road was a steep drop-off that went down to a creek. Eddie and I used to climb down that too. It was the local dump where everything was trashed; including dead animals etc. We would snoop through the dump and find lots of usable "goodies," like old silverware, dishes, cups, pots and pans. We would take them home and Ma would clean them up and boil them to make sure they were clean, and then we would use them.

If you turned left by the watering trough, it would take you down a one lane road to a wooded area with a nice stream and pond. We would go fishing there sometimes. I remember Eddie, Esther, Lloyd and the Coleman kids and me going there for a picnic on sunny days. I must have been about fourteen then. I wonder if they remember it?

THE OLD WATERING TROUGH

IT'S A PLANE!

When I was young, there was nothing flying in the sky except birds, bees, butterflies and an occasional kite some kid was playing with. Airplanes were just something out of the funny papers.

Mary, Tyke and I along with some of the neighbor kids were on our way to the Lee Center Fireman's Field Day, when we heard this sputtering motor noise in the sky. It was an AIRPLANE! It was like sighting a UFO today. Well, it landed in our pasture up by the woods. We all went running and whooping as fast as we could go to see what it was…

It had an open cock-pit and the pilot got out to fix something on the engine or whatever. He was dressed in the kind of outfit we saw in the "funnies" and even wore a helmet and scarf. Buck Rodgers???

He picked us up and let us look inside. We had to be extremely careful where we stepped as the wings were made of wood covered with canvas.

He was on his way to the Fireman's Field Day to try and interest people in taking a fifteen minute flight around the town for $5.00. When he started the plane he had to spin the propeller until it started. A lot like cranking a car. It was such a thrill for us to see a real plane, and to look inside it.

FIREMAN'S FIELD DAY

Our "Fireman's Field Day" was a big event. There were tents and stalls set up out in a big pasture past the school house. There were all kinds of "try your luck" stalls and a big tent, I don't remember if they had animals in there or not. When people won at the ring toss, shooting gallery, and others, the prizes were celluloid dolls, teddy bears, etc. and gold fish in a bowl. (When Lloyd got old enough to go to the Field Day, he was a whizz at winning the gold fish bowls!)

There were also hot-dog and hamburger stands and soda-pop and beer for the adults.

There was a very tall pole that was covered from top to bottom with axel grease. It had a $5.00 bill tacked to the top, as a prize for whoever could climb to the top. It was the Savoc boys who usually won it.

There was a baseball diamond where the men and boys played in the afternoon with bleachers for the crowd to sit on near it.

There was a one-armed man, Louie Bartlett; he lived across from the school house. He was one of the best pitchers they had. Sometimes they had "donkey-baseball" where the players rode on donkeys. That was really funny.

Firemen from Taberg came with their engine and had a water fight with the Lee Center firemen. It was fun to watch them falling down and slipping and sliding from the force of the water from the hoses.

Quite a few of us local kids would go there early the next morning to clean up the field. It was more like a treasure hunt. We found coins and sometimes dollars on the ground, especially under the bleachers. When we found some money we dashed over to Clyde Felshaw's or the Red and White store in town for candy and ice cream.

I don't know if they still observe Fireman's Field Day in Lee Center anymore. The last one I attended wasn't anything like they had in the old days.

FIREMAN'S FIELD DAY

"MYESTRO"

One day, when I was twelve or thirteen, I found a baby robin. It didn't have feathers yet. I don't know if it was pushed out of the nest or if I took it. Anyhow, I told Ma I found it on the ground. I found worms and bugs for it. I split a match half way up and held the food with that, and poked it down his throat like the mother bird does. He survived and grew big and thought he was one of us. He would eat with us at the table hopping from plate to plate for a handout.

When he started to fly, he was free to come and go as he pleased, but he never strayed far from home. I would just have to call "Myestro" and he would come flying to me, no matter where I was. I took him everywhere with me. He would ride on the handlebars of my bike. He would even ride on the tractor seat behind Pa when he went to plow the fields. He'd hop down behind the plow and get the worms etc. that the plow un-earthed. When he had enough he would come flying home.

I had a pair of blue and white spectator shoes which he hated. I don't know what was going on in his bird brain, but he would make a clapping sound with his beak and attack my feet when I wore them.

I thought he would fly away in the winter, but he didn't. I built him a nest out on the sun porch where he slept; he would come inside for meals with us.

I don't know when he got brave enough to visit the setting hen that Ma had, but he got a little too close one day and she pecked him to death. Broke my heart! We all missed him.

GRANDPA CANNON

Grandpa Cannon, Ma's father, died on May 11, 1941, he was almost 102 years old. We kids had never met him, but Ma told us stories and kept him in our minds like we really knew him. I know that she kept in contact with him in the Soldiers' Home in Wisconsin. She also kept in touch with her brothers and sister, Adeline.

When he died Ma and Stillman inherited $500 each from him. They couldn't wait to hot-foot to Rome to spend it. Probably before Pa could sweet talk her out of it.

I don't recall what Ma bought for all the other kids, but she bought Mary a pair of shoe ice-skates, I got a reversible coat, brown plaid on one side and the other a light tan, for when it rained, I also got a green corduroy skirt with red lining. I think that it was from Sears.

When we went to Monkey Ward's store, Still asked me if there was a bicycle that I liked. I didn't think I would really get it, but there was a really pretty aqua and cream colored one that caught my eye. I sat on it and it was a girl's bicycle, with a headlight and tail lights when I put the brake on. It had a bell on the handle bar that was used as a horn. And he bought it for me on the spot! Last of the big-time spenders!!!!!

I rode it for several years. The only thing was that Ma made me share it with the other kids and it wasn't long before it was beat-up and battered. It was still ride able though. I don't know how long it lasted Eddie, Esther and Lloyd.

OUR "HOMEMADE" MAKE-UP

When Mary and I were in our early teens, we decided that we wanted to wear make-up. Of course, Ma wouldn't hear of it. So, when Ma was gone somewhere, Mary would boil some sugar and water to "soft-ball" stage. Then she would light some matches until they burned out. She would scrape the black off the ends and add it to the sugar. That made good mascara, and was easy to wash off.

Instead of butter we had oleo. They call it margarine today. It looked a lot like lard, and came with a packet of orange powder, to mix in with oleo and make it look more like butter. Mary would open the powder and we would rub some of it on our cheeks and lips.

We saved our makeup until we were away

from home. I don't know what Mary kept it in. We must have had waxed paper. We would put it on when we went to Lee Center, where the other girls were allowed to wear makeup. We must have looked ok as no one said anything to us. We had to spit in the mascara to make it useable, but the other girls spit in theirs too.

CHARLIE EVANS

The Evans family lived up the road from Beckley's out of Lee Center, just before you got to Joe Yaworski's Bar. He was one of the characters that I distinctly remember. His little sister Pearl adored him and followed him everywhere and he enjoyed "showing her off." She was only three or four years old at the time. He would tell us she could eat just about anything we could think of. I remember when he caught a moth and said "Pearl will eat it, just watch." And sure enough, she did. Along with that she ate fish-worms, ants and butterflies. I don't remember what happened to her when she grew older, but they were quite the side show when we were growing up.

CHARLIE EVANS

PAINT-ON STOCKINGS

During the war no one could get silk or cotton stockings anymore. They had to use the material for the military. Pa and Ma's friends, Bill and Sue Rimkus from Ohio, would visit us every summer. They would leave Gramma Rimkus, Bill's mother, and their daughter, Dolores, at our place for about a month, while they went on their vacation.

Bill always gave Dolores spending money.

One day, she and I decided to walk to Lee Center and get some paint-on stockings. She was about eight and I was eleven. She bought it and we painted it on, a pencil came with it, to draw a line up the back of our legs to make it look like the seam. All of the women were wearing them.

When we decided to go home, it started to

rain. Oh! Oh! Pa was driving in to town and he saw Dolores and me all scrunched down with our dresses covering our feet. He stopped to see what the heck the matter with us was and did he ever have a good laugh when he saw what we were up to. We were squatting down and waddling our way home so the rain wouldn't wash our "stockings" off. He reminded us about that episode for years.

Dedication
This book is dedicated to Adam and Erin.
My inquisitive grandchildren who asked all the questions of my childhood years.
And to my loving family and friends who made these stories possible,
most of whom have passed on now, but "Oh the memories I keep deep inside."

Intermedia Publishing Group

Publishing That Works For You

Do you need a speaker?

Do you want S.T. Sweeney to speak to your group or event? Then contact Larry Davis at: **(623) 337-8710** or email: **ldavis@intermediapr.com** or use the contact form at: **www.intermediapr.com**.

Whether you want to purchase bulk copies of *Hayseed* or buy another book for a friend, get it now at: **www.imprbooks.com**.

If you have a book that you would like to publish, contact Terry Whalin, Publisher, at Intermedia Publishing Group, (623) 337-8710 or email: twhalin@intermediapub.com or use the contact form at: www.intermediapub.com.

PAINT-ON STOCKINGS